Then & Now
CHATTERIS

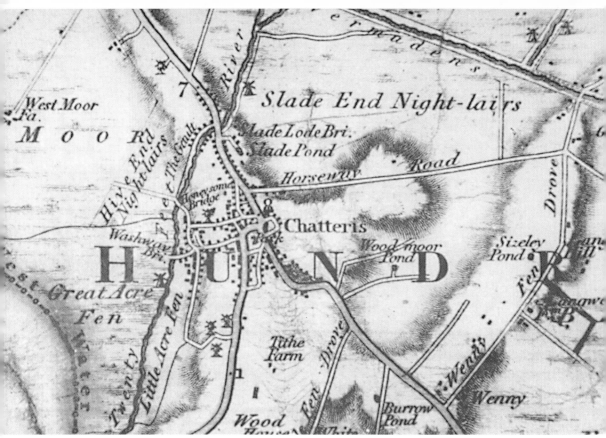

A map of 1830 showing Chatteris and the surrounding area. Note all the old names which are still used and the number of windmills which helped so much with fen drainage.

L. Wise.

Then & Now
CHATTERIS

COMPILED BY RITA GOODGER

TEMPUS

First published 2000
Copyright © Rita Goodger, 2000

Tempus Publishing Limited
The Mill, Brimscombe Port,
Stroud, Gloucestershire, GL5 2QG

ISBN 0 7524 2088 7

Typesetting and origination by
Tempus Publishing Limited
Printed in Great Britain by
Midway Clark Printing, Wiltshire

Chatteris Railway Station in the first half of the nineteenth century. Apart from the disappearance of the large chimney the station remained largely unchanged until it was closed in 1967.

CONTENTS

ACKNOWLEDGEMENTS

The author wishes to record her sincere thanks to the many people who have been such a great help in the compilation of this book - people who have lent photographs, taken photographs, allowed access to their property and provided facts and figures, including: The Bailey family, Bartletts, J. Bateman, I. Buckland, C. Cornwall, A. Ingram, G. Kightley, M. Kurton, J. Lenton, B. Limbrick, H. Mattock, G. Meeks, D. Oakey, F. Payne, J. Peggs, N. Rickwood, C. Seward, S. Stacey, M. Stokes, C. Thrower.

In 1977, the year of the Queen's Silver Jubilee, it was also the Golden Anniversary of the Womens' Institute. The local Womens' Institute decided to have a town sign designed, made and presented to Chatteris to mark this double celebration. The shield-shaped sign links the Bishops of Ely through the crowns; the lower section depicts a plough as a symbol of the towns most important industry - farming. The eels were included as at one time they were used for the payment of taxes.

INTRODUCTION

Many written opinions of Chatteris are not kind, 'it is ugly,' 'its long main street is cluttered and dreary,' 'an insignificant town which cannot be called attractive', to quote but a few. Maybe on short acquaintance you would agree; a plain High Street, a much restored church, unremarkable houses all surrounded by the flat fens. However living here one notices the little things that are usually not mentioned, the odd thatched house, the small weekly market with no more than half a dozen stalls, bright with colourful pot plants, buckets of flowers, vegetables and fruits in glowing colours, and the fish stall from Kings Lynn where you can buy crabs, whelks, cockles and mussels, and in season green and succulent samphire - the poor man's asparagus. There is the old elegant early Georgian house in Park Street, built for a farmer, which then became for many years the local post office. Built into several cottages and garden walks are pieces of stone, which is all that is left of a Benedictine Nunnery founded in 980AD; and set in a wall in Victoria Street is a scratch dial.

Chatteris, once a small market town in the Fens, has over hundreds of years gradually increased in size. This period has been packed with history and changes, especially during the twentieth century. The purpose of 'Chatteris Then and Now' is to illustrate the changes that have occurred within the community; changes to bricks and mortar and as well as to the social and economic welfare of its people.

Situated in the middle of these fertile fens Chatteris has always had important links with agriculture. The prosperity of farming has been based on crops such as sugar beet, potatoes and carrots. In the inter-war period Chatteris firmly established itself as the centre of the country's carrot growing industry. This crop, which for many years had been grown mainly for feeding animals became a nutritious and popular ingredient of our diet, containing vitamin C which supposedly helped one to see in the dark - this if true could have been a help in the 'black-out'!

The Agricultural Revolution brought about a total change in the lifestyle of thousands who lived by the land, the effects lasting until the middle of the twentieth century. Rural communities had relied totally on the landowners and the fruits of the land for their livelihoods and survival. The last forty to fifty years have seen hundreds of jobs disappear over the county with no end in sight to this downward spiral. A field which once needed dozens of people to sow, tend and harvest its crop, now needs the odd man helped by the latest machinery.

After the Second World War the draught horses gave way to the tractor and combine harvesters of ever increasing power and sophistication. Vast machines and sprays were capable of doing the work of gangs of men and women. Then came the increased demand for pre-packed vegetables and this provided alternative employment, as did the road transport industry which was needed to get produce to markets in London, the Midlands and the North. High cost of capital equipment has encouraged the formation of co-operatives, these need stronger and more organized marketing, so two successful enterprises now thrive - Fenmarc which grows and markets roots crops and Fengrain which stores and markets grain.

The ability to travel more easily reduced the isolation of the district, and improved road conditions created opportunities for workers to travel to neighbouring towns for employment in manufacturing and commerce. Growth in higher technology manufacturing in Cambridge and other accessible towns resulted in many inhabitants commuting daily – some even to London as the rail services improved. Although the railway station closed in 1967, Huntingdon, a main line station, is only fifteen miles away.

The 1901 Census gave the population of Chatteris as 4,711; in 1991 this figure had risen to 7,260. The greatest change shown during these years was the number of people employed in agriculture. This went from being the main occupation in 1921 when 50.6% of males worked on the land, compared with the figure today when only 340 members of the total work force are farm workers.

So the close knit community of large families started to split as the younger generation were able to leave home for further education or to seek employment in other parts of the British Isles, and today in other parts of the world. Their place is taken by older folk, who tired of the hectic life in urban areas choose to move into a country area where the pace of life is so much slower. Another attraction is the lower cost of housing so people retiring from a large town can sell their property and benefit financially when they settle here.

The town itself has also changed. As the improvement in the economic conditions of working people continued they had more money for motor cars, coloured TV's, electrical appliances of all kinds, foreign holidays and money for refurbishing and modernising their homes. Shopping became the great pastime and as people went out of town to seek a wider choice the local shops suffered, and family businesses closed as younger members of families no longer saw a future in the town. Some new owners taking over shops retained the old name but we now have new shops such as Breakers, Kids Stuff and Bodylines, and names like Weedons, Sharpes, Graham and Fisher have completely disappeared. Gone too are the public houses with names connected with farming, however in the main street we still have the old inns - The Cross Keys and The George, although the Ship is now renamed Walk the Dog. The once popular fish and chip shops (there is one left, run by the Petrou Brothers in West Park Street) have been replaced by a Chinese take away and an Indian Fast Food restaurant.

In the year 2000, Chatteris is being improved, road, pavement and street lighting are all being upgraded. Humps in the road, belisha crossings and countless road signs will all help to make Chatteris a safer place. But really it is the people who live here who make Chatteris such a friendly, welcoming and happy place in which to settle - or visit. With thriving organizations catering for all ages and tastes everyone can take an active part in the life of the town. We are so fortunate that many newcomers are willing to take their share and hopefully all the changes taking place will benefit future generations of Chatteris residents.

Rita Goodger
2000

Chapter 1

CHURCHES

The Salem (Particular Baptist) church was started in the 1800s by the two Clarett sisters. The church was attended by Antinomians who were people who denied the obligation of moral law. They believed that Christians were emancipated by the Gospel to keep the moral law, faith alone being necessary. This building, called the 'Old barn chapel' was replaced in 1907.

The Parish church of St Peter and St Paul was enlarged and restored in 1910. It had already been completely rebuilt after the Great Fire which destroyed most of the town in 1310. Over the years the fabric of the church has been maintained and improved but sadly in 1984 Chatteris lost one of its most imposing landmarks. The horse chestnut tree on the right of the picture, which for more than a century had dominated the paths leading from Market Hill to the church, had to be removed because it had a fungus disease which had affected its trunk. In the modern photograph a new view of the ancient place of worship has been opened up, giving Chatteris an enviable open forecourt for the Parish church.

The church, originally built in 1352, has been restored many times, but the galleries and box pews which appear in photographs taken in 1900, may have been put in around 1720 judging by an old account of materials used at that time. They were however removed in the early 1900s and replaced with wooden chairs, which rotten with woodworm, have recently been replaced by solid comfortable padded chairs. With a polished block wooden floor, improved electric lighting and adequate gas fired heating, the church of St Peter and St Paul is home not only to the regular services but to many other functions.

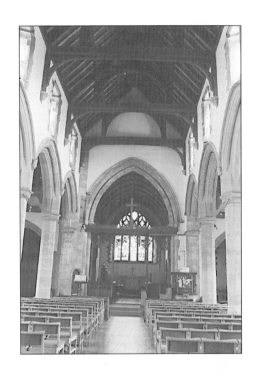

Although there has been a church in East Park Street for over one hundred and sixty years, this church was built and opened in 1838 and was known as the Congregational church. There was no front entrance, and the two side doors led into narrow aisles which were difficult to negotiate at special services such as weddings and funerals. In 1990 with falling numbers and the increasing expense of maintaining large churches, the Methodists, Baptists and Congregationalists (then the United Reform Church) decided to unite and meet in the United Reform church to be known as Emmanuel church. Since then fund raising has been continuous and successful and the building is now modernized with a centre entrance and modern facilities inside.

The members of Emmanuel aimed to provide a church building which welcomes and invites people. To do this they opened up the front of the church, replaced wooden pews with chairs that can be moved, in order to create a multi-purpose and flexible church with internal corridors so that people can move from one area to another without having to go outside. The church is available for bookings by the public and is used by many organizations for a variety of events, concerts, bazaars, sales, youth group functions, keep fit classes, lunches and dinners. Choir practices are all also held there. On Sundays the religious services are taken by the resident pastor which in the year 2000, up until September, was the Revd Brian Harley, when sadly he left to work as a hospital chaplain in Lincoln.

WESLEYAN CHAPEL, CHATTERIS.

T he Wesleyans built their church in New Road in 1815, later becoming Methodists. In 1903 they built a Sunday School on the opposite side of the road. Eventually they closed the church, the property was sold and with additions was used as a vegetable packing factory. The Methodists continued to worship in the Sunday School until they joined with other denominations at Emmanuel church in East Park Street. This site was bought by local medical practitioners who sold off the front area to a housing company who built Swan House - a nursing home for the elderly which contains forty single en-suite rooms with all necessary accommodation features and available services. The barn on the left of the photographs, which belonged to the farmer next door, is still standing today though it has been converted into a comfortable four-bedroomed house.

The Star Supply Store on High Street. The assistants, always immaculately dressed in their white coats and long aprons, pose with their manager. The photograph shows a typical shop window in the period after the Second World War with the prices of all the goods clearly marked. This is the shop where Mr W. Cowley trained before starting in his own business; he can be seen second from the right.

This photograph shows the White Hart Public House at the corner of Huntingdon Road and West Park Street in the process of being demolished as part of a road improvement scheme. Originally built well over a century ago, the pub was burned down at the end of the nineteenth century. When rebuilt it was run by various landlords including Mr Fysh, Mr Collins, Mr Hosken and Mr Clarke. The widow of Mr Clarke remained there until the pub was closed. Today the pleasant garden area is owned and maintained by the Fenland District Council.

Situated at the end of Park Street at the junction with Station Road and West Park Street, this house and shop were occupied for many years, and throughout the Second World War, by the Sinden family. Mr Charles Sinden, a cabinet maker by trade had a wonderful tenor voice and was always in demand for concerts. He formed and trained the Chatteris Choral Society as well as a Women Institute choir. This shop had a very commanding position and was ideal for decorating at Christmas. Mr W. Dring, the last owner, carried on as a draper and grocer. Demolished early in 1960 the cottages on the left were replaced by a house (now used as offices) and a blank wall fills the gap. In the old picture the sign can be seen pointing to the Chatteris Station but today's picture shows the arrow pointing the opposite way to the A141.

The people of Chatteris were very excited when a new modern cinema was built in the 1930s and the two nightly performances and a matinee on Saturdays were always well supported. Unfortunately the Empress Cinema, along with many others up and down the country, was forced to close as with the development of the television, people no longer felt the need to go to the 'flicks' so frequently. The cinema was purchased by Percy Rooke a local builder who changed its use to what it is today - a swimming pool. The front of the building is a showroom and at this time can be seen selling second-hand furniture.

Park Street, and the large house on the right was used as a post office until recently when all counter business was moved to the end of a stationer's shop in the High Street. This building is still used as a sorting office and here the local postmen and postwomen meet to collect the mail before cycling off to do their deliveries early in the morning. The trees have disappeared, as have the small cottages. In their place is a garage forecourt displaying cars for sale.

J. H. SCOTNEY

WILL'S's GOLD FLAKE CIGARETTES · WESTWARD HO! TOBACCOS · CAPSTAN NAVY CUT CIGARETTES

For many years this shop in Park Street was the main gents hairdressing establishment in the town. Many men visited regularly for a shave and 'lather boys soaped the chins of the customers ready for the master barber to whip round with a cut throat razor'. At the door we see Mr H. Scotney with his wife who helped in the business, and Mr M. Palmer their assistant at this time. Today the shop is a general store run by Ian Benny and is a handy place to call in for a newspaper, a bottle or something in the bakery or grocery lines and you might even buy a winning lottery ticket or scratch card!

In an agricultural town when the farmers relied on the 'horse', the harness makers were always busy. Whether the farm workers were ploughing or harrowing, all machinery and carts were pulled by horses. The Brewer family who started this business in the late nineteenth century carried on through four generations, branching out into leather work and sports equipment as the farm machinery became mechanized. Although the shop is still connected to transport it now has a totally different use as a Travel Centre, run by Mr John Watchhorn who is an agent for many national firms. Here you can book a holiday to wherever you wish, using whatever mode of transport you choose -a valuable service for a small country town.

This is part of the town which over the years has changed very little although of course shops have changed hands and goods sold have kept up with modern requirements. Fitches, the first shop on the right, was for years the main shop selling bicycles. Whether you wanted a new or second hand bicycle, or if you had a puncture you went to see Mr Fitch or one of his sons who helped in the business. Eventually the business was taken over by Mr and Mrs T. Tilley who retired in July 2000 and handed the business over to Mr Corney and his son-in-law. Further along, the harness makers' shop is now a florist, and outside the stationers' shop are black metal posts for protection. Flags decorate the High Street as it is Festival Week.

The Wilderspins were a Chatteris family and Fred Wilderspin is seen here standing in front of the shop that he took over in 1900. At that time he was a wheelwright and coach painter and even kept a horse to be let out with a coach. He went on to sell cycles and then motor cycles before selling his first Morris car in 1926. Eventually the business was carried on by his son Roy who worked there until he retired. Roy had joined the firm in 1947 when he was demobbed from the army. Today the old shop has disappeared, the forecourt has changed and petrol is no longer available for the public. There are however some garage services available although part of the premises is used for the selling of second-hand goods.

Rowell and Sons, originally a gentlemens' tailoring shop which had several changes of use during the twentieth century before being demolished and replaced by a block of flats. As can be seen, several of the other buildings have survived further down the street, even the old chimney stacks, although no doubt there are no open fireplaces in the houses today. In the new picture a 'sleeping policeman' can be seen in the road - a popular traffic calming measure although unpopular with local motorists.

In the 1920s Mr Clarke, seen here with his son, had a large jewellers shop in the High Street. He specialised in watches and clocks and employed a watch mender to help with repairs. This was a popular shop which carried a vast range of goods which were in demand for Christmas and wedding presents. He increased his business by starting a small library at one end of the shop, managed by his wife; the books could be borrowed for two pence a week. Today the modernized shop has an entirely different use – called 'Breakers' it is part of a big clothing company which caters for the young and 'with it' members of our community selling clothes which are fashionable and reasonably priced.

This picture was taken in 1954 at the junction of High Street and New Road. Many of the buildings disappeared long ago. Walker Stores in the centre of the picture is now Bonnetts the Bakers and next to it is the Salvation Army Charity Shop. To the right is the DIY shop. There are still buildings on the left which house a second hand furniture business. To the fore is the old ambulance station which has now been demolished and the land has been used for private development. The buildings on the right were also demolished and the area is now used as a sales area for used cars.

John and Martha Laws had five sons and three daughters and they lived in Railway Lane. John paid £100 so that his son Alfred could serve his apprenticeship to a butcher in Kettering. He returned to Chatteris, and having married, opened a butchers' shop in High Street. He regularly travelled by train to St Ives market to buy cattle, and the drovers then walked with his purchases to Chatteris, to await slaughter in the abattoir at the end of his back yard. In 1930 the original butchers' shop was pulled down and rebuilt with a clean looking white tiled frontage. In 1946 he sold the business to Roger and Lena Collins. Today the shop has disappeared and No. 54 High Street is a house, the home of Mr and Mrs G. Palmer.

As the number of car owners increased so the day out shopping became more popular, this was the beginning of the run down of local businesses. However for most people the local weekly shopping was still done in Chatteris, especially when groceries could be delivered by the errand boy. In the old photograph is Mr W. Cowley, a quietly spoken kindly gentleman, in his shop in the High Street. He lived in the flat above with his wife and daughter. Although there were six grocers within a short distance, business was brisk. Probably his most popular item was the cooked ham he prepared himself - a great favourite with farm workers for 'dockey' or high tea. After Mr Cowley retired, Jack Mitchell started a jewellers business. Today it is a cycle shop run by Bob Gowler who is seen here in front of many aids to cycling; he also sells everything you need to enjoy the sport of fishing.

At the north end of High Street was one of the largest stores which was run for many years by partners Samuel Lovell and James Ward. The shop had several departments - grocery, drapery, millinery, furniture - and was considered to be 'the shop' for local ladies to buy the latest fashions. The business, taken over by the Penfold family in 1952, was moved up the street to smaller premises and concentrated on selling furniture and bedding. This picture shows the shop windows of Lovell and Ward advertizing the sale before the business moved. The whole site was purchased by the local authority making it possible in 1977 to improve yet another busy road junction and

design a garden in which was incorporated a town sign designed for and donated by the local W.I.

On the left of the old picture is a baker's shop. The house next to it was for many years the home of the Parkinson family. Mr Parkinson was one of several undertakers in the town during the 1920s, although today there is only one. The house was demolished and replaced by a modern store - Somerfields. Fenland District Council in upgrading the town, have re-paved the front of the shop, installed railings and a Belisha crossing, which has made it safer for folk to cross the road.

Mr and Mrs Arthur Mason with their apprentice, nephew Reg Setchfield, outside their shop in High Street. They sold furniture at a time when transport was difficult and people setting up home preferred to buy locally. Their shop was a converted house, but apart from a name board over the front door, the front remained unaltered for many years. Eventually a large shop window was inserted and business flourished until the Second World War at which point people had to be satisfied with utility furniture. The house on the right is still standing complete with the lovely bow window over the door. On this site a road now leads down to new estates of bungalows and houses, and a warden controlled complex - Quaker Way – which is run by Fenland District Council.

As the Co-op movement grew in the inter-war period, the people of Chatteris along with people all over the country, benefited from the lower prices on offer. With several departments including a drapery, butchery, grocery and furniture department, people joined the movement and by giving their number whilst shopping they were able to collect sizeable dividends. Here we see some of the assistants in front of the shop in the 1930s. Today the building is just a plain looking block of flats, although there is still a Co-op in the town – Pioneer - on the outskirts of town which is a very large spacious store all the facilities for parking and shopping which is expected these days.

The White Mill down London Road was used for grinding corn. When the large barn next to the Mill was demolished it was found to have the date of erection of 1788 inscribed on it. The house to the left of the picture, now occupied by the Peggs family, has been modernized. Mr Peggs has built a garage using some of the old bricks including the stone with the date from the old mill building. Today a new estate has been developed - Whitemill Road, although the old house to the left is still the original one.

This large family house in South Park Street with its fine porch and stone steps leading up to the heavy front door has disappeared along with the stone wall. The stones were part of the perimeter wall of Chatteris Abbey which was closed in 1538, having been in existence for some five hundred years. Yet again the space has been filled by modern housing.

The Market Hill, Chatteris, has undergone a certain amount of change and improvement. Hiltons shoe shop has had various occupants, including a cleaning agency and a financial advisor, although when the modern photograph was taken, the premises were empty. The bus, supposedly the first one to appear in Chatteris, the carts, pedestrians and gossiping cyclists all indicate how quiet and unhurried life was at this time. Dr Nix's house on the right was replaced in the 1960s with a pleasant garden where people can sit and watch the world go by.

A large dwelling in St Martin's Lane - 'The Shrubberies' - was last occupied by Mr Stuart Richardson and his family. It was demolished in 1964 to make way for a new housing development. The new road is named 'The Shrubbery' and these bungalows are popular because they are so near to the centre of the town.

Chapter 3
INDUSTRY

A field of leeks, a popular fen vegetable. This crop was sown, cultivated and harvested by hand.

modern picture shows the complicated machinery which is used to wash and grade carrots today, inside the works of Albert Bartlett & Sons Ltd. This business, established in 1945 took over a Chatteris firm in 1960, and they are today the largest producers of parsnips, carrots and onions in the United Kingdom, supplying supermarkets the length and breadth of the country. They currently grow over 1,000 acres of onions, 500 acres of parsnips and 2,000 acres of carrots. Customers need a continuous supply so when local produce is not available they import from other countries, for example parsnips from Israel and Spain or onions from New Zealand and Chile.

After the Second World War carrots became the main crop grown in the Fens, and they provided work for many agricultural workers. After digging up the carrots with forks they were topped and washed with water pumped from a nearby drain. The

Approaching Chatteris across Acre Fen by the A142 from Huntingdon, the flat fen road with its splendid avenue of poplar trees, and the surrounding fields, were enhanced on this December morning by a coating of crisp sparkling snow. As can be seen by the modern photograph this approach road has changed dramatically. The poplar trees have long since gone - it was apparently impossible to keep the road level and safe with shallow tree roots spreading in from the verges on either side. Today the fields have been developed by the firm A.R. Bartletts which is one of the largest vegetable packing firms in the British Isles. It is no longer a quiet peaceful fen road, as lorries, tractors and cars arrive at all hours of the day and night.

Quite close to the centre of the town, the Rickwood family had a large yard where sheds were erected for storing and packing vegetables, keeping other farming equipment, such as carrot washers and haystackers. Here we see sacks of carrots ready to be taken to the railway station for transport to markets all over the country. With the coming of road transport and the entirely new way of harvesting and packing root vegetables, the site was no longer required by the farmer. Sold to a private developer, we now see a spacious and pleasant development of houses and bungalows. Conveniently placed, this is a popular estate especially with older folk. The name of 'The Hawhorns' reminds Chatteris folk of a very popular vicar, the late Revd J. Hawthorn who was in charge of the church from 1938-1975.

This is Mr Moulton on the first potato harvesting machine which he invented and had made at his Engineering Works in Chatteris in the early 1900s. Pulled by four horses, it was later adapted and propelled by a simple steam engine. It was sent for trials to other parts of the country but unfortunately the soil was not light and peaty as it is in the Fens. As a result the engine was unable to pull the harvester, it got stuck and exploded - so this was the only part of the country where this machine was used. The modern harvester is much more powerful and efficient, this one harvests two rows at a time and is used by Mr Richardson in Langwood Fen.

Ploughing matches were held regularly in the Fens, and Arthur Maycock seen here was a champion ploughman. The three shire horses belonged to the late Alderman Leonard Childs and they could plough one acre a day. Fen horses were always driven on a single rein, and being well trained would answer to a steady pull or a series of jerks with the accompanying voice command of 'Woke up' meaning turn to the left or 'Gee oh' meaning turn to the right. Their leather harness would be well oiled and supple with polished brasses gleaming in the sun, and on special occasions with tinkling bells and coloured plumes. A modern tractor which has replaced the horse can be used for pulling all kinds of machinery and loads, and now up to forty acres can be ploughed in one day.

Gone is the time when the farm labourer would go out to work in the fields soon after dawn, wearing his old clothes, his wellies tied round his ankles (the poor man's gaiters) so that no mice could run up his trouser legs. He would take his dockey with him, usually a hunk of bread and a slab of cheese washed down with a bottle of cold tea. In this picture, harvest is over and the hay is stacked. Now, when harvest time comes, one meets the huge mechanized combine harvesters, moving from one farm to another where they cut wide swathes through the fields, thresh it and deliver the grain into bags on a platform at the rear of the machine. The sweat and toil have gone but the dust remains.

The tunnel under this bridge once drained water from the west of the town. Eventually, with a changed water system the water in the tunnel dried up and for a time the land leading into the tunnel was used for allotments. With the growth of pre-packed locally grown vegetables, factories sprang up, and on this site Whitworths built an office block on stilts. Today vegetables from all over this area are sent to Chatteris to be sorted and packed and then despatched to markets and chain stores all over the country.

The West Park Street Baptist chapel was built towards the end of the 1880s but with falling numbers and high costs it closed in 1990, its members then joining other congregations to worship at Emmanuel church in East Park Street. After standing empty for a while the chapel was purchased by Mr S. Davies. The outside view looks virtually the same today so the modern picture shows the interior which has changed considerably. The wooden pews, the pulpit and the organ have all been removed, a new staircase runs up the centre of the building linking the two floors, as the now level balcony has been extended. Mr

Davis furnishes show houses, so rows of stacked shelves almost hide any remaining old features although glimpses of the windows and beautiful wooden ceiling can still be seen.

Early in the twentieth century there were two breweries in the town, Lindsells and Morgans, and further beer was delivered by horse-drawn drays from breweries elsewhere. This picture shows a group of workers in front of Lindsells Brewery which closed in 1926. The property was bought by Charles Cole who re-sited his small Engineering Works which he was running in London Road. His boast was that he could make anything from a darning needle to a traction engine. Today we have Lindsells Walk, and a new block of flats now stands on the site which once provided employment for so many Chatteris people.

In 1851 Chatteris had an estimated population of 5,000 and had 15 inns and hotels with a further 43 beer houses. Many of the small ale houses had their own brews which no doubt varied according to the water used, whether it was spring or well water. This is the King William IV, the last landlord was Mr J. Stacey who took it over in 1936 when mild beer was 4d a pint, bitter beer 6d a pint and whisky 12s 6d a bottle. Today beer is only produced locally in Chatteris by Dr Thomas who has a small brewery on the Dock Road Industrial Estate and supplies the surrounding area with his local brew.

Mr F.W. Seward started an auctioneering business in 1891. In the early years of the twentieth century auctions were held at the White Lion but in 1917 he bought Chatteris House for a family home and later his son Lindsey joined him in the business. The auction yard was next to Chatteris House and the Friday weekly auction of fruit, vegetables and furniture was well supported. This auction could take up to nine hours and the record number of eggs sold on one day was 1,250 score! In the older photograph you can see Lindsey with his wife and sons John and Colin at the very last auction held before the business closed in 1970 when Lindsey retired. As a valuable site in the centre of the town the buildings were demolished to make way for yet another housing complex - Old Auction Yard.

In 1847 a train line was opened from Cambridge, through St Ives and Chatteris to March. Many people used this line to travel to work, especially to Chivers Jam Factory at Histon. For a time these factory workers had special uncushioned compartments in case their clothes were sticky! The railway became very important to the average person - it was the main means of transport for many years and was used for holidays, days out, and to take Chatteris children to school in March. Mr Caton, the last station master lived in the Station House with his family, but left when the station closed in 1967. Today the site belongs to the Cambridgeshire County Council, and was used for a while as a local highways

depot and refuse dump. The modern photograph shows an empty and derelict site, but in September 2000, the go ahead was given to open an industrial site with associated offices.

The Chatteris Engineering Works started trading about 1900 and the business grew steadily - being situated next to the railway station was a great help. As diamond and gold mining developed in South Africa, orders for machinery came to Chatteris and goods were crated for dispatch by rail and sea. Later the name of the firm changed to stainless metal craft and new types of machinery were produced. Two steel towers were exported to Sweden to become part of a fuel refinery, and aluminium air separation columns were made for British Oxygen – they were 106ft long, and weighed 45 tons. Today the works have been added to and modernized, much of the work being planned on computers. Body scanners for our hospitals are a popular product today, and the work force is still over 100.

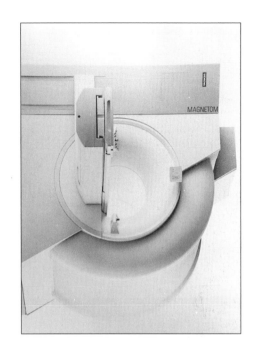

The Engineering Works produced cranes in the inter-war years, which were then sold to all parts of the British Isles. The one pictured is on the harbour at Ryde, Isle of Wight and is still in use today. Attached to it is a plate saying where it was made. Today one of the main products of the Works is the scanner and these are supplied to many hospitals.

Leaving Chatteris by Wenny Road you would once have come to a very popular public house - The Five Bells. People would take a walk or a bicycle ride on a summer evening or at the weekends, to sit and gossip over a pint of ale. This old picture was taken one Sunday lunchtime when the landlord, together with a neighbour and his family, posed with other customers who have arrived on their bicycles dressed in their Sunday suits and collars, ties and caps. Today the public house has been replaced, and back from the road now stands a modern bungalow which has appropriately been named the 'The Five Bells'. The five bells can be seen in the front door panel. This is now the home of the Wing family who run a successful haulage firm.

Mr T. Russell, an agricultural worker, took this snap of his wife with their daughter, twin sons and his brother in front of their house in London Road in the 1920s. The house and surrounding land has been purchased by David White and with his family he runs a very successful garden centre, which is popular for miles around as gardeners visit for an enjoyable few hours. The house is now a restaurant run by Mary Mullis and her sister and hot meals and snacks are available. One day a week senior citizens belonging to the Gardening Club at 'D.J's' meet for a talk or demonstration.

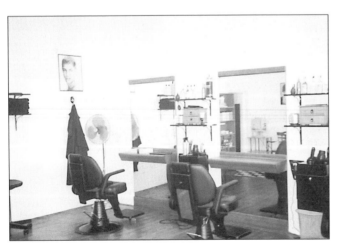

This Park Street pharmacy was run by the Dwelly family from 1868-1940. A shop full of shelves and drawers of all sizes, these jars held such items as Glauber Salts, Epsom Salts, powdered Liquorice, Tartaric Acid, Cream of Tartar, Salts of Lemon etc. Today the interior is changed completely as Kevin Morris has a gents hairdressing business known as 'The Cutting Gallery'.

Richard Mandley, John Laws and David Laws trying the stocks on a school visit to the local museum in 1959. Last used in 1820 they were wheeled to a public place so all could see a culprit being punished. The sentence was imposed by the local magistrates and they were only used for men. Women were put on a 'ducking stool' and ducked in the nearest river or pond.

Chapter 4
SCHOOL DAYS

When Cromwell School was opened in 1938 it had many 'ordinary' classrooms, rooms where the rows of desks would seat some thirty plus pupils. Gradually the desks were replaced by tables and forms moved round the school to lessons in the appropriate subject room. This still happens but all the rooms are now completely different, carpeted, and with all the new apparatus and technology available as education advances. The music room seen here gives the students a chance not just to sing but to learn to play percussion instruments and electronic equipment as they study all forms and sorts of music.

In 1938 Cromwell School opened with separate departments for boys and girls. The only day of the year they shared was Sports Day. Here we see Miss G.M. Judge, headmistress, on the left and Mr J. Llewelyn, headmaster, holding the shield which is about to be presented to the captain of the winning house by one of the governors. Today the college is co-educational but the same shields and cups are presented. Although distances and weights vary the girls now have all the same events as the boys - even a tug of war.

School concerts have always been popular and for many years consisted of a varied programme of musical and dance items with one act plays. Lines were learnt and well rehearsed and most of the staff helped in some way with scenery, props, make-up, costumes, lighting, business arrangement or with the producing. From left to right: Roger Peachey, Roger Edgeley, Garry Garner, Rosemary Casey, Elaine Purrell, Robin Pell, Derek Clarke.

Today at the local Community College most of the shows produced are musicals and here we see four couples from the last show 'Shaking not Stirring'. From left to right: Victoria Rayner, Robert Cooke, Aimee Garner, Bradley White, Natasha Drayton, Ben Watson, Kate Howlett, Mark Heading.

In 1959 a party from the Cromwell School visited Boppard in Germany. This was the first of many educational visits arranged by staff. Full uniform was worn except in the evenings and visits to places on interest, beauty spots and local industries were arranged. Before evening dinner notes were written up and checked by staff. On returning, a parents evening was arranged so all could enjoy a full account of the visit and see scrapbooks, souvenirs, photos and the cine film collected. The earlier photograph was taken outside Cromwell school just before the party left for an educational visit to Switzerland in the 1960s. Nowadays trips from Cromwell are usually to enjoy leisure activities, and here is a group of students on a skiing trip.

The first Hive End Infants School was built in 1873 and then rebuilt in 1888 at a cost of £325 to accommodate 138 children. In 1904 it was enlarged to take 207 pupils and from 1928 was able to take infants who had previously been taught at the New Road Infants School. Eventually a new infants school was built at this end of the town in the Burnsfield area, and Hive End became a Community Centre in 1960, closing in 1993 due to its unsafe condition. The County Council sold the land, part of it going to the Freemasons as their hall was adjacent and they needed land for a car park. The rest of the space was sold for housing development.

Rounders is a team game which is played by juniors and seniors. Played with the same shaped wooden bats it is sometimes a pleasant change to see the 'Then' and 'Now' pictures so much alike even though many years have passed. The 'Then' team had to play in the King Edward School playground bounded by roads which must have been a problem. Today the new school in another part of the town has spacious grounds in which to enjoy all outdoor games and sports.

The small building was the first infant school to be built at the north end of the town. The tall building behind it was the local workhouse and is now a block of flats. When a new school was built to cater for increased numbers, Slade Lode School was sold by the County Council to the local Boxing Club. Eventually the interest in boxing waned and today the building is derelict, waiting for the new owner to make plans for the use of the site. The best parts are the wrought iron works on the front wall! With Burnsfield Infants School and King Edward Junior School still unable to cope with increasing numbers, another school - Glebelands - has been built off New Road. This new school is large, airy and spacious and can take over 300 infants and juniors.

The Corn Exchange on Market Hill became a cinema and was renamed the Picture Palace. Bought by Mr Herbert Barrett in 1938 it had another change of use and became a dance hall. A new oak floor attracted dancers from far and wide and besides the weekly dances it was used by many organizations for a variety of functions. A visiting hypnotist booked the hall and here we see a packed audience enjoying the show. Many were hypnotised and with hands locked above their heads had to join the hypnotist on the stage to get help!

Chapter 5
LEISURE AND ACTIVITIES

A proud day in the 1930s when the district colours were dedicated in the church - a service attended by all members of the Guide Movement in Chatteris. The officers, from left to right: The Hon. Mrs de Beaumont (county commissioner), Lady Brackenbury (divisional commissioner), Mrs F.A. Barrett (district commissioner). Standing behind the officers: Miss E. Warth (headmistress of Westwood House, a local private school), District President and Miss H. Warth (member of staff of the King Edward Junior School), District Secretary. The Brownie uniform was plain brown with a brown woolly hat. Today the uniform is much more colourful and exciting.

The 2nd Chatteris Guide Company was reformed during the last war. Meeting weekly in Cromwell School they enjoyed many activities, such as tracking on a summers evening, and cooking supper over a camp fire. They also studied and researched to take interest badges which when won were proudly displayed stitched onto the sleeves of their uniform. Having passed the Tenderfoot Test they were enrolled which was a memorable occasion when they took their Guide Promises and also promised to keep the Guide Laws before a trefoil guide badge was pinned on their tie by an officer. The uniform was a straight long sleeved navy cotton dress, large brimmed felt hat and a triangular folded tie which could be used as an arm sling during first aid practices, and a shiny brown leather belt completed the outfit. Today the uniform has completely changed to a modern bright 'with it' casual style - Headquarters have designed uniforms which they hope will attract Chatteris youngsters.

Formed in 1927 the local branch of the Women's Institute has held its meetings in various halls. As numbers increased it became the largest branch in the British Isles and at this time meetings were held in the Palace.

Even so no more than 400 could be accommodated and there was a waiting list. After being very active during the war - making jam, canning fruit, selling meat pies, and helping at all local functions and catering for some old people who were evacuated from a home in London - the members finally settled down after the war to their normal pursuits. These included entering drama and music festivals, attending craft classes and generally improving their home making skills. Today the WI still flourishes, though the membership is smaller, and the members still appreciate the friendship, entertainment and the various speakers and demonstrations as well as functions where they meet up with neighbouring groups.

In 1967 a very active group was formed in Chatteris, a branch of a National movement for 'Business and Professional Women', known as the B & P. With enthusiasm it took part in all town and national activities and supported many charities. A choir was formed by the members, trained by Georgie Goodall with Gillian Young as pianist, and this was much in demand, and entertained frequently at local functions. Sadly, thirty years later in 1977 the club closed - the number of members, about fifty, had remained constant but with pressure of modern life it became more and more difficult to find ladies with time available to run the branch. Members of the choir from left to right, back row: Mrs A. Seward, Mrs D. Ibbott, Mrs G. Young, Mrs J. Tilley, Mrs B. Munns. Middle row: Mrs J. Jones, Mrs J. Margetts, Mrs S. Shipp, Mrs P. Bailey, Mrs H. Francis, Mrs

G. Goodall. Front row: Mrs M. Griffith, Mrs R. Goodger, Mrs M. Markwell. However, the following year with the help of several newcomers to the town, a branch of Townswomen's Guild was formed, and although numbers are small, lively monthly meetings are held at the Cromwell Community College.

fixtures in the season and take part in league games. Here we have the Chatteris Town Football Club in 1947, they now have grounds in West Street with full facilities for their social life. During 1999 a Chatteris Town Youth Football Club known as the Fen Tigers has been formed. A Chatteris boxing hero Dave 'Boy' Green, a national champion, was known as the Tiger and he is the president of the club. They have 250 members of both sexes and hold training sessions on Saturdays and play in league fixtures on Sundays. They have their own grounds in Wenry Road known as 'Peacock's Paddock as the land was donated to them by Bob Peacock a retired farmer'.

Football has always been a very popular game and pastime in Chatteris, teams have their own grounds with supporters clubs to back them. They have regular

The energetic Ladies Football Team, 1949. From left to right, back row: Mrs Overall, Mrs Peachey, C. Congo (coach), J. Seekings, Mrs Scott. Middle row: Mrs Lewis, Mrs Fuller, Mrs Grummit, R. Kightly, Mrs Fuller. Front row: J. Adams, S. Adams. Today the game still attracts the girls – the modern photograph shows members of one of the girls teams which belong to the Chatteris Town Youth Football Club.

The start of a family outing in the early days of motoring. This Model 'T Ford' had solid tyres, it was not a comfortable ride but it was exciting for the privileged few who could afford this new luxury. Today we are spoilt for choice - so many shapes, sizes and colours, all available with countless extras - power steering, air bags, automatic gearbox, central locking, child locks on doors, electrically controlled windows, air conditioning, radio and cassette player. This small 'W' Reg four seater is being filled with unleaded petrol which at the time was just under £4 a gallon, petrol for the old car was $7\frac{1}{2}$ old pence a gallon!

Motorbikes appeared at the beginning of the twentieth century, hard tyres and poorly sprung seats didn't provide a very comfortable ride. There were no special suits but with a cap worn backwards the young men of the day enjoyed a slow ride through the countryside. Today we see Sean King in his padded leathers and crash helmet, which today is a legal requirement, riding his Yamaha Virago. This is one of the smaller models available, a 535cc which does 45 miles to the gallon and can reach 105mph. The largest model available is 1800cc and can do 215mph. For Sean it is a leisure activity, he has just completed a sponsored ride for local charities from John O'Groats to Lands End, some 2180 miles.

People from all walks of life keep and race pigeons. For many years racing pigeons were transported by rail. Today, they are conveyed either by 'Road Transporters' which can hold up to 6,000 birds, or by air. Racing takes place from April until September, and a bird weighs about one pound. They can fly at speeds of just over 40mph on a quiet day and reach up to 110 mph with a back wind; the most miles flown on one day is 75. In the older photograph Jack Bateman can be seen in front of his loft holding 'Ramblers Pride' the winner of a race from Lerwick in the Shetlands, some 535 miles. Today there is more interest taken in Cage Birds, and the Cage Bird Society in Chatteris holds regular meetings and shows; this is one of the keenest members, Bill Watkinson, at home with his collection.

Hospital Sunday, an annual event enjoyed by everyone. A parade headed by the Town Band is followed by members of the UDC, decorated floats from various organizations and local youth groups carrying their colours. The whole parade was also accompanied by countless collectors, rattling their wooden boxes as they collected for the local hospital. Most of the town folk turned out to watch and finished up in the local recreation grounds and Manor Park to have an afternoon of fun. Although this event has been discontinued, Chatteris now holds a festival, usually a whole week in July when town events are arranged: barbecues, discos, an art exhibition, a flower festival, quizzes, displays, musical concerts and many other functions when people raise money for their own organizations and for charities. The 'Chatteris in Bloom' festival is held

during this week and local gardens are opened in aid of the Arthritis Research Campaign and many people enjoy walking round. This picture was taken in the garden of Mr and Mrs R. Negus of London Road who ran a draw, proceeds going to a hospice in Cambridge.

For many years a queue of men waiting to sign on the dole was a common sight. Farm work was seasonal so many families relied on dole money, especially in the winter. The Labour Exchange at one time was in the front room of Mr W. Seaton's house in Park Street. When larger premises were required a site was bought in South Park Street - an old house and buildings were demolished, and a new Labour Exchange was built. In 1975 this was sold when other methods were found to deal with the unemployed. It was brought by Mr Stuart Stacey who adapted it and opened it as a Public House, The Honest John. Today the pub has been enlarged and modernised and is a popular venue for eating and drinking, with a large room available for organizations to hold functions.

The first mention of bowling in Chatteris appeared in a list compiled by the Cambridgeshire County Bowling Association in 1899. Since then the sport has gradually gained popularity, particularly with ladies. The Chatteris Town Bowling Club is situated in Wood Street. Beginning with an old green wooden building consisting only of a mens' changing room and toilet, with a space for machinery, it was later adapted and ladies facilities were added. In 1948 an old army hut was purchased and erected as the club pavilion and a kitchen was added. This was replaced in the 1990s and with it came an increase in membership. Today, during the playing season it is a hive of activity. There are open weekly drives, friendly matches with other clubs and one day competitions for trophies donated by former members, including Doris Skinner, Jean Pearson and George

Austin. There are also knock-out competitions leading to finals as well as league matches. The bowler in the recent picture is Eric Laws when at the age of ninety-two he played in the celebratory centenary match having been a member of the club for fifty years.

The Chatteris Town Band was formed towards the end of the nineteenth century. Dressed in military style green uniforms they played mainly church music at the beginning, branching out into marches when they became a marching band. Much in demand locally they headed parades and gave concerts, not only in Chatteris but in neighbouring towns; they particularly enjoyed engagements in Hunstanton and Yarmouth. In the 1950s they won many prizes in contests and became the Chatteris Silver Prize Band; they still enter the regional and national competitions. They have been fortunate in receiving a grant of £40,000 from the Lottery to buy new instruments, and donations from the local Rotarians and Court Leet to purchase new uniforms. No longer an 'all male' band they welcome not only ladies but youngsters who are interested in music and they play all kinds of music from jazz to classical. However they are no longer a marching band and the marching drums are housed in the local museum.

This substantial detached dwelling is brick built with a tiled roof. Built in 1910 it has an unusual Dutch style gable end and had many other attractive features throughout, including gas lamp brackets, ceiling friezes and decorative door mouldings. Dr O'Connor the first owner took a great interest in its construction, he wanted it to look old so mud was smeared on the outside bricks, oak beams were collected from old mills for the hall, and stones from the nunnery were used for the front wall.

Chapter 6
HOUSING

Another curious feature of the streets of Chatteris are the 'yards'. These are mostly groups of tiny cottages which were quickly run up for agricultural labourers in the nineteenth century. They were built round a small open space or 'yard', so that each group could use a communal tap and lavatory. A stranger would probably not notice them at all since they usually lie behind narrow openings leading off the main streets. Here we see Charlie Angood making his weekly collection for the Salvation Army in the Co-op yard, now Pecks Yard. In the modern day picture there is a modern development of flats bungalows and houses erected by private developers.

Lyons Yard off Park Street contained some twelve small cottages with communal facilities. Here we see the Oakey children in front of their home. In the 1920s one of the cottages was adapted and a fish and chip shop added - the most popular 'buy' was 'one and one' comprising of one piece of fish dipped in batter and fried in dripping and a portion of chips. These were wrapped in a small piece of white paper and then in newspaper - all for three old pennies. Today we see a modern warden controlled complex named 'Lyons Court', built and managed by the Fenland District Council which contains single flats and bungalows for couples in the grounds

001 Salem Chapel, Chatteris

This Salem chapel was built in 1907, and although there was a fire in 1922, it was repaired and services were held there until 1968. In 1972 the property was bought by the Dolby Bros. for residential development. Part of the land was sold to the Fenland District Council who built a warden controlled complex for senior citizens. There are twenty-nine flats, twenty-six of which are one-bedroomed and two are adapted for disabled people. The warden is Mrs G. Mayes, a Chatteris person who returned to Chatteris with her husband after a career in nursing. She is a member of a well-known Chatteris family - her father was the late Joe Smith, JP, a very prominent and useful member of the community.

Chatteris House in the centre of the town was built in 1828. Large and imposing it has a portico porch sheltering a fine doorway with an iron balcony above. Inside the house was a stone curved stairway with an iron balustrade. For many years it was a family house but eventually it was sold and altered, the windows were enlarged and it became first a grocery store and then a restaurant. Unfortunately at the time this picture was taken it had stood empty for a while and had been vandalised. Today it is being prepared for yet another use - a residential school for twenty-nine children, aged seven to eleven, who are currently in care from all over the country.

So many servicemen who had married during the war, needed housing once they had been de-mobbed. Councils up and down the country bought prefabricated bungalows and quickly erected them section by section expecting them to fill the gap possibly for ten to twelve years until they could be replaced by something more permanent. Erected in 1946 in St Martins Lane and costing £150 8s (40p) a week to rent, the Chatteris prefabs went on and on and were not removed until March 1993 - then very carefully, section by section, so they could be sold on to use in other buildings. Tenants moved into caravans nearby as bungalows of similar shape and size were built (for Fenland District Council) by Jack Chambers a local builder.

From the late nineteenth century these old cottages housed Chatteris families - usually agricultural workers. With no indoor facilities people were very ready to move as the houses became more dilapidated. They were purchased and demolished by the UDC. In their place small attractive bungalows were built for pensioners. A service road runs round the back but in the front on Wenny Road they have a pleasant grassed area.

A unique old house which stands at the gates of the first cemetery in New Road. It is no longer used by the cemetery keeper, as both the Chatteris cemeteries are serviced by Fenland District Council. The house is unusual as it is the only one in Chatteris faced with granite. The small girl with her bicycle is Grace Meeks, the daughter of the last cemetery keeper to live there. Today the house is let by the council. This relatively new house was built by David Green, a Chatteris lad who became a national hero in the boxing world. Large and comfortable with a swimming pool at the back, the house can be recognised by the concrete boxing gloves on the pillows of the front wall.

A blacksmith's shop stood at the top of St Martin's Road and was owned at one time by the late Mr Frank Heading. The last blacksmith to work there before its closure was Mr L. Kightly. At that time there were five blacksmiths in town shoeing horses. Mr Kightly carried out repairs of all kinds, in particular to the farmers' carts and wagons. Today in the place of the forge stands a modern detached house named 'The Forge'.

Westwood House was for many years the home of the banker Sir William Clarke and his daughter Winnie. On his death it was sold to the Warth family who opened it as a private school. The pupils became a familiar sight in the town with their maroon gymslips and blazers, with Panama or velour hats, and maroon and gold striped ties and hatbands. When the school closed it was sold and the new owner demolished the cumbersome building and replaced it with a modern house. Today it is the business premises of the solicitor Gordon Cartwright.

A golden wedding group, taken over seventy years ago, of the Rickwoods, a well-known Chatteris farming family. Arthur Rickwood (second from the left on the back row) undertook a lot of public work especially in local government - at one time he was High Sheriff of Cambridgeshire. He made his fortune growing carrots and it is strange that today the biggest farmer in Chatteris, John Heading, who has just completed his year as High Sheriff, grows a variety of crops but no carrots at all.

Chapter 7
SERVICES

town. In 1931 the first lady was elected and this photo was taken outside Grove House, the first council offices owned by the town. From left to right, standing: Mr A.S. Rickwood, Mr C.T. Hammerton (rate collector), Mr S. Barrett, Mrs F.A. Barrett, Mr E. Gautrey, Mr H. Heading, Mr L. Childs. Seated: Mr S.M. Haigh (surveyor), Mr J. Gage (vice-chairman), Mr W.E. Seaton (chairman), Mr C. Dobb (clerk), Dr R.E. Nix (Medical Officer of Health). Today meetings are still held on the first Tuesday of each month. Having purchased the old surgery in Church Lane there are rooms available for hire for other organizations such as the CAB. The town museum is also housed in this building.

Chatteris was administered by the UDC from 1894-1974. The town is divided into four wards, and every three years an election is held to appoint nine members to represent the

Mr Charles Dobb became clerk to the Chatteris UDC before the Second World War and stayed in that position, until local government reorganization in 1973 left Chatteris with a parish council which had very little power, and nowhere near enough work for a full-time clerk. Mr Dobb worked in Grove House, sitting at a large table, his telephone on the shelf behind him and the room heated by a gas fire. He knew every corner of Chatteris and apart from his love of bowls his whole life was dedicated to the welfare of Chatteris and its inhabitants. Today the parish council is once more the town council and has a part time clerk. Joanna Melton, a mother of four and the wife of Alan, the present county councillor for Chatteris, works at the council offices in Church Lane in an office fully equipped with all the modern equipment that is so necessary today. A small rate is levied and included in the Fenland District Council rate but the town council are only responsible for small local matters.

The police station in East Park Street stands next to the Salvation Army Citadel. When first built, part of the building was used by the officer in charge and his family to live in. There was also a court room which was used regularly by the local magistrates to try cases, cells to lock up the odd criminal or drunk, and offices for the police on duty. Today we see a modernized building, all of which is used by the police on duty in the area. The local people can only contact the station for short periods - at other times they have to ring the March Station or the Police Headquarters at Hinchingbrooke.

The friendly policeman that so many remember, patrolled the town on foot or rode his bicycle in his navy uniform and helmet. With no means of communication he would carry two pennies in his pocket just in case he had to call into the station from a telephone kiosk in an emergency, his only weapon a wooden truncheon. Today our community policeman PC Rolfe has the use of a police car and is in constant touch with his headquarters to be able to call for assistance and receive it at short notice.

The old fire station was a small building in front of the church. The horses to pull the equipment were fetched from their daily work of pulling the dustcart which collected the town's refuse. Today our fire brigade has a purpose built station near the centre of the town. There is room on-site for training and all the equipment is up to date so that they are prepared for any emergency at short notice.

At this time there were four fire crews attached to the fire station and each one had a messenger. One crew was on duty each night and had to sleep at the station. This meant that most weeks, two nights were spent on duty by each crew. In 1942 the messenger relay team pictured (S. Stacey, W. Brown, F. Fayes, B. Fuller) entered a relay area championship competition and won this cup. The framed items are diplomas won at other competitions. After the Second World War the air raid siren alerted the firemen during the day but after 10 p.m. bells rang in their houses. Today each fireman carries an alerter which tells him when he is needed on duty.

The Cambridgeshire County Council first opened a library in Chatteris in a classroom at King Edward School. Books were stored in boxes and one evening a week the books were spread on the desks for selection by the public. As the demand for reading material grew, a permanent base was found in part of the girls school in New Road. The Cromwell School had been built and this old school was used as a Youth Centre, but the building was old, so was eventually demolished and a prefabricated building was erected on the site to house the library. Today we have this large modern library in High Street, built in conjunction with the Fenland District Council, and part of the building is used by the Fenland District Council Housing Department.

The old gentleman is Joe Lamb, smartly dressed for a family wedding. During the 1920s he was the Town Crier. When any event needed publicising he would ride round the town on his bike stopping at street corners to ring his hand bell and in a thunderous voice shout his message. Such events might include an important town function or maybe when the water was to be turned off for a repair to the mains. At other times he had a barrow which he trundled round the streets selling his goods - usually fruit and vegetables. With his family he lived in Burnsfield Street. When his son died he left a substantial sum of money to form the Lambe Trust Fund. Every Christmas the interest is divided between any OAPs living in Burnsfield Street. The other gentleman is Reginald Wenn - Wenn the Pen as he is known. Although confined to a wheelchair he makes his

presence felt. Scarcely a week passes without a letter from him appearing in the local press. Any problem or trouble in the town and Reg brings it to everyone's attention – especially to the local authorities. He is also a prolific writer and has published several books of poetry, the proceeds of which are given to help different charities. Always willing to help he speaks to various organizations - a very kindly and generous gentleman.

L ife was much easier for the housewife before the last war – bread and milk were delivered daily and the fish merchant and green grocer appeared down your street at least once a week. Often the grocer would call for your weekly order and deliver later on the same day. Here we see Ernie Kightley, a local handicapped young man who trundled round the town every day selling fruit and vegetables. Today the main commodity you can purchase outside your home is ice cream. This van rides round Chatteris at the weekend playing a tune and stopping to serve youngsters who rush to queue for ice cream in all shapes, sizes and flavours.